Wolverhampton Wandere

101 Questions To Test Your
of Wolverhampton Wan....

Published by Glowworm Press
7 Nuffield Way
Abingdon OX14 1RL

By Chris Carpenter

Wolverhampton Wanderers Football Club

This book contains one hundred and one informative and entertaining trivia questions with multiple choice answers. With 101 questions, some easy, some more challenging, this entertaining book will test your knowledge and memory of the club's long and successful history. You will be asked a large variety of wonderful questions on a wide range of topics associated with Wolverhampton Wanderers Football Club for you to test yourself.

The book is packed with information and is a must-have for all loyal supporters. You will be quizzed on players, legends, managers, opponents, transfer deals, trophies, records, honours, fixtures, songs and more, guaranteeing you an educational experience and hours of fun. Informative and enjoyable, this Wolverhampton Wanderers Quiz Book will provide the ultimate in entertainment for all Wolves fans and will test your knowledge of **Wolverhampton Wanderers Football Club** and prove you know your Wolves trivia in this addictive quiz book.

2020/21 Season Edition

FOREWORD

When I was asked to write a foreword to this book I was flattered.

I have known the author Chris Carpenter for many years and his knowledge of facts and figures is phenomenal.

His love for football and his skill in writing quiz books make him the ideal man to pay homage to my great love Wolverhampton Wanderers Football Club.

This book came about as a result of a challenge in a Lebanese restaurant of all places!

I do hope you enjoy the book.

Colin McDonald

Let's start with some relatively easy questions.

1. When were Wolverhampton Wanderers founded?
   A. 1875
   B. 1877
   C. 1879

2. What is Wolverhampton Wanderers' nickname?
   A. The Baggies
   B. The Saddlers
   C. The Wolves

3. Where do Wolverhampton Wanderers play their home games?
   A. The Kennel
   B. Molineux
   C. Sunbeam Stadium

4. What is the stadium's capacity?
   A. 32,005
   B. 32,050
   C. 32,500

5. Who is the club mascot?
   A. Wibbly
   B. Wobbly
   C. Wolfie

6. Who has made the most appearances for the club in total?
   A. Steve Bull

B. Kenny Hibbitt
C. Derek Parkin

7. Who is the club's record goal scorer?
    A. Steve Bull
    B. Billy Hartill
    C. John Richards

8. Who is the fastest ever goal scorer for the club?
    A. Steve Daly
    B. Derek Dougan
    C. John Richards

9. What song do the players run out to?
    A. Hi Ho Silver Lining
    B. The Happy Wanderer
    C. The Wanderer

10. Which of these is a well known pub near the ground?
    A. The Apple Tree
    B. The Feathers
    C. The Vine

OK, so here are the answers to the first ten questions. If you get eight or more right, you are doing very well so far, but the questions will get harder.

A1. The team were founded as St Lukes in 1877 after a headmaster at St Lukes Church in Blakenhall presented a football to some pupils. Two years later they merged with local cricket and football club The Wanderers to form Wolverhampton Wanderers.

A2. Wolverhampton Wanderers nickname is of course the Wolves.

A3. Wolverhampton Wanderers play their home games at Molineux, and have done since 1889.

A4. The current stadium capacity is 32,050.

A5. The club mascot is Wolfie, and in recent times he has been joined by a female mascot - Wendy - who we believe is the only mascot in English football with a handbag, so give yourself a bonus point if you mentioned Wendy.

A6. Full back Derek Parkin has made the most appearances for the club. He played in 609 first-team matches from 1968 to 1982.

A7. Steve Bull is Wolverhampton Wanderers' record goal scorer with 306 goals in all competitions.

A8. On the 15th November 1975 John Richards scored just 16 seconds after kick off in Wolves' 5-1 romp at Turf Moor, Burnley.

A9. The players run out to Hi Ho Silver Lining. The song, which was recorded by Jeff Beck, dates back to 1967. As a little bit of trivia for you, Rod Stewart sang backing vocals on the recording.

A10. There are many pubs near the ground, but The Feathers is perhaps the most well known. Be prepared to queue for a pint though.

OK, back to the questions.

11. What is the highest number of goals that Wolverhampton Wanderers has scored in a league season?
    A. 109
    B. 115
    C. 121

12. What is the fewest number of goals that Wolverhampton Wanderers has conceded in a league season?
    A. 25
    B. 27
    C. 29

13. What is the highest number of points Wolves have managed in a season?
    A. 101
    B. 102
    C. 103

14. Who has made the most league appearances for the club?
    A. Kenny Hibbitt
    B. Derek Parkin
    C. Billy Wright

15. Which stand is considered the 'traditional' home end of the ground at Molineux?
    A. Steve Bull
    B. Stan Cullis

C. Jack Harris

16. What is the club's record attendance?
   A. 61,135
   B. 61,315
   C. 61,513

17. Where is Wolverhampton Wanderers'
   training ground?
   A. Bodymoor Heath
   B. Finch Farm
   C. Wolves Training Ground

18. What is the name of the road the ground
   is on?
   A. Liverpool Street
   B. Paddington Avenue
   C. Waterloo Road

19. Which stand has the biggest capacity?
   A. Steve Bull
   B. Stan Cullis
   C. Billy Wright

20. What is the size of the pitch?
   A. 109x70 yards
   B. 110x71 yards
   C. 112x72 yards

Here are the answers to the last ten questions.

A11. Wolverhampton Wanderers scored an incredible 121 goals in 42 matches in the Second Division in the 1930/31 season.

A12. Wolverhampton Wanderers conceded just 27 goals in 40 matches in the First Division in the 1987/88 season.

A13. It's a staggering 103 points in a season, which was achieved as Wolves finished champions of League One in the 2013/14 season.

A14. Derek Parkin with a staggering 501 league appearances holds the record for the most league appearances for the club.

A15. The "traditional" home end of the ground is now occupied by the Stan Cullis stand - what used to be known as the "North Bank" back in the days before all seater stadiums.

A16. Wolverhampton Wanderers' record home attendance is 61,315 against Liverpool on 11th February 1939.

A17. Wolves Training Ground, near Chapel Ash, is the catchy name of the training ground.

A18. The official address for the stadium is Waterloo Road.

A19. The Billy Wright Stand has the largest capacity, being able to accommodate 8,608 people, all seated.

A20. The size of the pitch is 109 yards long by 70 yards wide. By way of comparison, Wembley's pitch is 115 yards long by 75 yards wide

Now we move onto some questions about the club's records.

21. What is the club's record win in any competition?
    A. 13-0
    B. 14-0
    C. 15-0

22. Who did they beat?
    A. Adam's Pottery
    B. Crosswell's Brewery
    C. Kipling's Bakery

23. In which season?
    A. 1886/87
    B. 1889/90
    C. 1902/03

24. What is the club's record win in the league?
    A. 8-1
    B. 9-1
    C. 10-1

25. Who did they beat?
    A. Coventry City
    B. Leicester City
    C. Manchester City

26. In which season?
    A. 1917/18
    B. 1927/28

C. 1937/38

27. What is the club's record defeat?
    A. 1-10
    B. 1-11
    C. 1-12

28. Who against?
    A. Bodymoor Heath
    B. Hampstead Heath
    C. Newton Heath

29. In which season?
    A. 1892/93
    B. 1902/03
    C. 1912/13

30. Who has scored the most hat tricks for
    Wolverhampton Wanderers?
    A. Steve Bull
    B. Derek Dougan
    C. Kevin Richards

Here are the answers to the previous block of questions.

A21. The club's record win in any competition is 14-0.

A22. The club beat Crosswell's Brewery 14-0 in the second round of the FA Cup.

A23. The match took place on 13th November 1886, so it was the 1886/87 season.

A24. The club's record win in the League is 10-1.

A25. The club beat Leicester City 10-1.

A26. The match took place on 15th April 1938, so it was the 1937/38 season.

A27. The club's record defeat in any competition is 1-10.

A28. It was Newton Heath who defeated Wolverhampton Wanderers 10-1. To give them their full name it was Newton Heath Lancashire and Railway Football Club. They changed their name in 1902 to Manchester United.

A29. The match against Newton Heath was played on 15th October 1892, during the 1892/93 season.

A30. Steve Bull scored a staggering 18 hat tricks in his time with the club. Legend.

Now we move onto some questions about the club's trophies.

31. When did the club win their first league title?
    A. 1943/44
    B. 1953/54
    C. 1963/64

32. When did the club win their first FA Cup?
    A. 1893
    B. 1923
    C. 1953

33. Who did they beat in the final?
    A. Everton
    B. Liverpool
    C. Tranmere Rovers

34. What was the score?
    A. 1-0
    B. 2-1
    C. 3-1

35. How many times have Wolverhampton Wanderers won the League?
    A. 2
    B. 3
    C. 4

36. How many times have Wolverhampton Wanderers won the FA Cup?
    A. 2

B. 3
C. 4

37. How many times have Wolves won the League Cup?
    A. 0
    B. 1
    C. 2

38. Who was the last captain to lift the League trophy?
    A. Stan Cullis
    B. Jimmy Mullen
    C. Billy Wright

39. Who was the last captain to lift the FA Cup?
    A. Norman Deeley
    B. Bill Slater
    C. Billy Wright

40. Who was the last captain to lift the League Cup?
    A. Willie Carr
    B. Andy Gray
    C. Emlyn Hughes

Here are the answers to the last set of questions.

A31. Wolverhampton Wanderers won their first league title at the end of the 1953/54 season.

A32. Wolverhampton Wanderers won their first FA Cup in 1893.

A33. Wolverhampton Wanderers defeated Everton at the Fallowfield Stadium in Manchester in the FA Cup Final held on the 25th March 1893.

A34. Wolverhampton Wanderers beat Everton 1-0, with a goal from Harry Allen.

A35. Wolverhampton Wanderers have won the League three times - 1953/54; 1957/58 and 1958/59.

A36. Wolverhampton Wanderers have won the FA Cup four times, the last time in 1960.

A37. Wolverhampton Wanderers have won the League Cup twice, in 1974 and 1980.

A38. Billy Wright was the last captain to lift the League trophy - in April 1959. Stan Cullis was the manager of that glorious Wolverhampton side.

A39. Bill Slater was the last captain to lift the FA Cup. He lifted the cup when Wolverhampton Wanderers defeated Blackburn Rovers 3-0 on 7th May 1995. Norman Deeley scored twice in the final and was voted man of the match. That season Wolves missed out on a third consecutive league title by just one point, coming second behind Burnley. Wolves also reached the quarter finals of the European Cup that season. Those were the days, my friend.

A40. Emlyn Hughes was the last captain to lift the League Cup after Wolves beat Nottingham Forest 1-0 in the final on 15th March 1980. The only goal of the game was scored by Andy Gray.

I hope you're having fun, and getting most of the answers right.

41. What is the record transfer fee paid?
    A. £25 million
    B. £30 million
    C. £35 million

42. Who was the record transfer fee paid for?
    A. Raul Jiménez
    B. Fabio Silva
    C. Adama Traore

43. What is the record transfer fee received?
    A. £14 million
    B. £27 million
    C. £41 million

44. Who was the record transfer fee received for?
    A. Steven Fletcher
    B. Matt Jarvis
    C. Diogo Jota

45. Who was the first Wolverhampton Wanderers player to play for England?
    A. Charlie Brown
    B. Charlie Chaplin
    C. Charlie Mason

46. Who has won the most international caps whilst at Wolves?
    A. Peter Broadbent
    B. Ron Flowers

C. Billy Wright

47. Who has scored the most international goals whilst a Wolverhampton Wanderers player?
    A. Ron Flowers
    B. Dennis Wilshaw
    C. Both Ron Flowers and Denis Wilshaw

48. Who is the youngest player ever to represent the club?
    A. Ron Flowers
    B. Jimmy Mullen
    C. Geoff Palmer

49. Who is the youngest ever goal scorer?
    A. Ray Goddard
    B. Gerry McAloon
    C. Alan Steen

50. Who is the oldest player ever to represent the club?
    A. Archie Gemmill
    B. Archie Goodall
    C. Archie Thompson

Here are the answers to the last set of questions.

A41. The record transfer paid by Wolves is £35 million.

A42. The record £35 million transfer fee was paid to Porto for Fabio Silva in September 2020. This eclipsed the previous record, £32 million which was paid to Benfica for Raul Jiménez in July 2019.

A43. The record transfer fee received by Wolverhampton Wanderers is £41 million.

A44. The fee was received from Liverpool for Diogo Jota in September 2020.

A45.Charlie Mason was the first Wolverhampton Wanderers player to play for England - in 1884!

A46. Billy Wright won 105 caps for England while he was at Wolves. Legend.

A47. Both Ron Flowers and Dennis Wilshaw scored ten times for England whilst they were Wolverhampton Wanderers players.

A48. Jimmy Mullen is the youngest player ever to represent the club. He made his first team debut at the age of 16 years, 43 days against Leeds United on 18th February 1939.

A49. Alan Steen is the youngest ever goal scorer for Wolverhampton Wanderers. He scored against Manchester United at the tender age of 16 years and 265 days in March 1939.

A50. Archie Goodall is the oldest player ever to represent the club. He appeared for the club at the age of 41 years and 116 days against Everton on 2nd December 1905.

Let's get onto the next set of questions.

51. Who did Wolfie the mascot once get in a
    punch up with?
    A. Foghorn Leghorn
    B. Red Riding Hood
    C. Three Little Pigs

52. Who is the club's longest serving manager
    of all time?
    A. Jack Addenbrooke
    B. Major Frank Buckley
    C. Stan Cullis

53. Who is the club's longest serving post war
    manager?
    A. Stan Cullis
    B. Bill McGarry
    C. Graham Turner

54. What is the name of the Wolverhampton
    Wanderers match day programme?
    A. Molynews
    B. Wolves Official Matchday Magazine
    C. Wanderers News

55. What is the club's official website
    address?
    A. thewolves.co.uk
    B. wolves.co.uk
    C. wwfc.co.uk

56. What is the club's official twitter account?

A. @TheWolves
B. @Wolves
C. @WWFC

57. Which of these is a Wolverhampton Wanderers fanzine?
    A. A load of bull
    B. The tatter
    C. Under a wanderers scarf

58. What animal is on the club crest?
    A. A dingo
    B. A husky
    C. A wolf

59. Who is considered as Wolverhampton Wanderers' main rivals?
    A. Aston Villa
    B. Birmingham City
    C. West Bromwich Albion

60. What could be regarded as the club's most well known chant?
    A. I was born under a Wanderer's scarf
    B. Stevie Bull's a tatter
    C. Those were the days

I hope you're learning some new facts about the club. Here are the answers to the last set of questions.

A51. Back in 1998, Big Bad Wolfie got into a scuffle with The Three Little Pigs, after they were telling a lot of porkies in a match at Ashton Gate against Bristol City. As Wolfie chased the piggies, the Wolves fans were singing "Wolfie's going to get you".

A52. Jack Addenbrooke is the club's longest serving manager of all time. He served from 1885-1922 and was in charge for a staggering 1,125 matches.

A53. Stan Cullis is the club's longest serving post war manager. He served from 1948-64 managing a total of 748 matches.

A54. The catchy name of the Wolverhampton Wanderers match day programme is 'Wolves Official Matchday Magazine'.

A55. wolves.co.uk is the club's official website address.

A56. @Wolves is the club's official twitter account. It tweets multiple times daily and has well over half a million followers.

A57. A Load Of Bull was the best known of the Wolverhampton Wanderers fanzines, but unfortunately it ceased publication in 2012. The Tatter is the most recent fanzine - and it is published eleven times a year.

A58. Wolverhampton Wanderers' badge consists of a stylised wolf's head.

A59. All three are rivals, but West Brom is of course the main rival.

A60. 'I was born under a Wanderer's scarf' to the tune of 'I was born under a wandering star' was huge in the 1960s and 70s but in more recent times "Those were the Days" can be regarded as the club's most well known chant. Altogether now...."Once upon a time, there was a tavern..."

Let's give you some easier questions.

61. What is the traditional colour of the home shirt?
    A. Gold
    B. Green
    C. Grey

62. What is the traditional colour of the away shirt?
    A. White
    B. Green
    C. Red

63. Who is the current club sponsor?
    A. ManBetX
    B. The Money Shop
    C. W88

64. Who was the first club shirt sponsor?
    A. Goodyear
    B. Manders
    C. Tatung

65. Who supplies kit to the club?
    A. Adidas
    B. Umbro
    C. Le Coq Sportif

66. Who is currently the club chairman?
    A. Sammy Chung
    B. Guo Guangchang
    C. Jeff Shi

67. Who was the club's first foreign manager?
   A. Tommy Soderberg
   B. Ole Gunnar Solksjaer
   C. Stale Solbakken

68. Which ex-player was the first black player to captain England?
   A. George Berry
   B. Sylvan Ebanks-Blake
   C. Paul Ince

69. Who was the top goal scorer for the 2019/20 season?
   A. Matt Doherty
   B. Raul Jiménez
   C. Diogo Jota

70. What position did the club finish at the end of the 2019/20 season?
   A. 7th
   B. 9th
   C. 11th

Here are the answers to the last set of questions.

A61. The traditional colour of the home shirt is of course gold, and it is complemented by black shorts. The colours come from the city's motto "Out of darkness cometh light", with gold and black representing light and dark respectively.

A62. The traditional colour of the away shirt is white.

A63. International gaming company ManBetX is the current shirt sponsor.

A64. Tatung was the first shirt sponsor of Wolverhampton Wanderers, back in 1982.

A65. Adidas is the current kit supplier to the club.

A66. Jeff Shi is the current club chairman.

A67. Stale Solbakkaen was the club's first foreign manager, who took over on 1st July 2012, and was sacked on 5th January 2013.

A68. Paul Ince was the first black England captain.

A69. Raul Jiménez netted 17 times in the league, and 27 times in total to become the club's leading goal scorer for the 2019/20 season.

A70. Last season, the club finished in 7th place in The Premier League. Considering the extended season and all the European games, that was very respectable.

Here is the next batch of ten carefully chosen questions

71. Wolves have played in all four professional divisions of the English Pyramid. How many of these divisions have they been champions?
    A. 2
    B. 3
    C. 4

72. In which season were Wolves last crowned champions of one of these divisions?
    A. 1988/89
    B. 1998/99
    C. 2008/09

73. Who did Wolves beat to win the Texaco Cup in 1971?
    A. Airdrie
    B. Hearts
    C. Motherwell

74. Molineux stadium got its name from whom?
    A. Barnabas Molineux
    B. Benjamin Molineux
    C. Bernard Molineux

75. On 24th June 2003, who played live to over 30,000 people at Molineux?
    A. Aerosmith

B. Black Sabbath
C. Bon Jovi

76. Who was the first manager of the club?
A. Jack Addenbrooke
B. George Jobey
C. George Worrall

77. What was the transfer fee paid for Ivan Cavaleiro by the club?
A. £5 million
B. £7 million
C. £9 million

78. How many goals did Derek Dougan score for the club in total?
A. 103
B. 113
C. 123

79. Who is regarded as the saviour of the club following his takeover in 1998?
A. Jack Hayward
B. Jack Walker
C. Dave Whelan

80. Where was Leander Dendoncker born?
A. Belgium
B. France
C. Germany

Here are the answers to the last set of questions.

A71. Yep, Wolves have been champions of all four professional divisions. A unique record at the time, which has since been matched by Burnley and Preston.

A72. Wolves were champions of the second division of the pyramid, known these days confusingly as The Championship in 2008/09.

A73. To win the Texaco Cup, Wolves beat Heart of Midlothian 3-2 on aggregate in the final. The crowd for the Molineux leg of the final was 28,462.

A74. The Molineux name originates from Benjamin Molineux, a successful local merchant. The family name derives from their original home in Molineaux-Sur-Seine in Normandy. The Molineux family first came to England in 1307 at a time when Flemish wool workers were teaching the British their trade. They chose to live in Wolverhampton, which in time became an important wool town. In the 18th century, a number of prosperous businessmen including Benjamin built fine, substantial houses near their place of work. As a result large Georgian houses appeared in Dudley Street, Victoria Street, Berry Street and Bilston Street, and the largest of them all was Molineux House. In 1860, the estate was purchased by O E McGregor, who converted the land into a pleasure park. Molineux Grounds, as it was titled, included an ice rink, a boating lake, and most crucially an area for football.

A75. Bon Jovi performed in front of 34,000 people at Molineux in what was, and still is, Wolverhampton's largest ever live concert.

A76. From 1877 to 1922, the team was selected by a committee whose secretary had the same powers and role as a manager has today. There were two secretaries during the period, George Worrall who was in charge for 4 games, whilst Jack Addenbrooke was in charge for an incredible 1,125 matches. Then in 1922, the club broke from this tradition and appointed George Jobey as the first full time manager.

A77. Wolves paid £7 million to Monaco for Cavaleiro in August 2016.

A78. After scoring a hat trick on his debut in March 1967, Derek Dougan scored 123 goals in 323 appearances including 95 goals in the league.

A79. Sir Jack Hayward saved the club in 1998. If it wasn't for him, who knows where Wolves would be now.

A80. Dendoncker was born in Belgium.

Here are the next set of questions.

81. In between the Billy Wright and the Jack Harris stands, there are 900 or so seats, known locally as what?
    A. The Gene Kelly Stand
    B. The Gene Sarazen Stand
    C. The Jean Genie Stand

82. What nationality is goalkeeper Rui Patricio?
    A. Brazilian
    B. Portuguese
    C. Spanish

83. How many goals did Steve Bull score in total in 1987/88?
    A. 44
    B. 48
    C. 52

84. When did Wolverhampton Wanderers reach the EUFA Cup Final?
    A. 1970
    B. 1971
    C. 1972

85. Whom did Wolverhampton Wanderers beat in the 1960 FA Cup Final?
    A. Blackburn Rovers
    B. Blackpool
    C. Burnley

86. How many Wolves players have won the Football Writers' Player of the Year award?
   A. 0
   B. 1
   C. 2

87. How many goals did Steve Bull score for England?
   A. 1
   B. 2
   C. 4

88. When was the last time Molineux hosted an England international?
   A. 1954
   B. 1956
   C. 1958

89. When did Jack Hayward gift his shares to Steve Morgan?
   A. August 2005
   B. August 2007
   C. August 2009

90. Who wears shirt number 15 for the 2020/21 season?
   A. Willy Boly
   B. Conor Coady
   C. Marcal

Here are the answers to the last set of questions.

A81. The temporary uncovered, open to the elements, stand is known as the Gene Kelly stand, as anyone who sits there will be "Singing in the Rain".

A82. Patricio is one of the Portuguese contingent at the club. He signed for Wolves in the summer of 2018.

A83. Steve Bull scored a staggering 52 goals in all competitions in the 1987/88 season.

A84. Wolverhampton Wanderers reached the UEFA Cup Final in 1972 losing 2-3 on aggregate to Tottenham Hotspur.

A85. On the 7th May 1960, Wolves beat Blackburn Rovers 3-0 at Wembley to win the club's fourth FA Cup final.

A86. Two Wolves players have been voted the Football Writers' footballer of the year:- Billy Wright in 1952; and Bill Slater in 1960.

A87. On the 27th May 1989, Steve Bull made his debut for England coming on as a substitute in a match against Scotland at Hampden Park, Glasgow. Naturally, he scored. He went on to earn 13 caps, scoring 4 goals for his country.

A88. Molineux has hosted four England internationals, the last of which was on 5th December 1956 when England beat Denmark 5-2 in a World Cup qualifier.

A89. Sir Jack Hayward gifted Wolverhampton Wanderers to Steve Morgan for a mere £10 in August 2007. As part of the deal, Morgan agreed to invest £30 million "for the benefit of the club". Sir Jack, we salute you.

A90. Willy Boly currently wears the number 15 jersey.

Here is the final set of questions. Enjoy!

91. When were Wolverhampton Wanderers relegated to the Second Division for the first time?
    A. 1926/27
    B. 1928/29
    C. 1930/31

92. In 1954, live on the BBC in one of those memorable floodlit matches, Wolves beat which famous Hungarian side 3-2?
    A. Debreceni
    B. Honved
    C. Ujpest

93. Who played for the Hungarians that night?
    A. De Stefano
    B. Eusebio
    C. Puskas

94. What shirt number does Conor Coady wear?
    A. 14
    B. 15
    C. 16

95. How many times did Billy Wright captain England?
    A. 70
    B. 80
    C. 90

96. Who started the 2020/21 season as manger?
    A. Nuno Esperito Santo
    B. Paul Lambert
    C. Walter Zenga

97. The Football League's first ever penalty kick was on the 14th September 1891. Which of these happened?
    A. Wolves were awarded a penalty, yet missed
    B. Wolves were awarded a penalty, and scored
    C. A penalty kick was awarded against Wolves, and it was scored

98. In which season did Wolverhampton Wanderers last win the First Division League Championship?
    A. 1956/57
    B. 1957/58
    C. 1958/59

99. Wolves have been managed by which former England national team managers?
    A. Glenn Hoddle
    B. Mick McCarthy
    C. Graham Taylor

100. Who is regarded as the most successful manager in the history of Wolverhampton Wanderers?

A. Sammy Chung
B. Stan Cullis
C. Graham Turner

101. Whose statues are present outside the ground?
    A. Steve Bull and Stan Cullis
    B. Steve Bull and Billy Wright
    C. Stan Cullis and Billy Wright

Here is the final set of answers.

A91. Wolverhampton Wanderers were relegated to the Second Division for the first time in the 1930/31 season.

A92. In what is recognised as the most famous game in the club's history, Wolves, as newly crowned League champions, came from 0-2 down to win 3-2 against Honved. After the game, one newspaper declared Wolves "Champions of the World".

A93. The Honved side boasted the legendary forward Ferenc Puskas.

A94. Coady wears shirt number 16.

A95. Billy Wright played 105 times for England, and the great man captained his country on 90 of those occasions.

A96. Nuno Herlander Simoes Esperito Santo started the 2020/21 season as manager, but more specifically Head Coach. He was appointed to the role in May 2017. All the best for this season, Nuno.

A97. Wolves were awarded, and scored, from the Football League's first ever penalty kick. How about that for a bit of trivia!

A98. The last time Wolverhampton Wanderers won the League was in the 1957/58 season.

A99. Both Glenn Hoddle and Graham Taylor managed Wolves; Taylor from March 1994 until November 1995 and Hoddle from December 2004 until July 2006.

A100. Stan Cullis is regarded as the most successful manager in the history of Wolverhampton Wanderers. Under his leadership, Wolves won the league title three times, were runners up three times, won the FA Cup twice, and also won the Charity Shield. The Wolves side of the 1950s were like the Liverpool side of the 1980s and the Manchester United side of the 1990s. He was a formidable man.

A101. The statues are of Stan Cullis and Billy Wright. The Billy Wright statue was unveiled in 1996 and along with Bobby Moore at Wembley and Peter Osgood at Stamford Bridge, it ranks in the top three football statues in the UK.

That's it. That's a great question to finish with. I hope you enjoyed this book, and I hope you got most of the answers right.

I also hope you learnt some new facts about the club, and if you saw anything wrong, or have a general comment, please visit the glowwormpress.com website.

Thanks for reading, and if you did enjoy the book, would you please leave a positive review on Amazon.

Printed in Great Britain
by Amazon

53578689R00028